Anchorage Times Dave Predeger

To General Brown
and Claudine Brown
with appreciation
and sincere affection.

Pio Laghi

March 9, 1984

POPE JOHN PAUL II

A Visit to Anchorage, Alaska

POPE JOHN PAUL II
A Visit to Anchorage, Alaska,
February 26, 1981

ST. PAUL EDITIONS

Printed in U.S.A. by the Daughters of St. Paul
50 St. Paul's Ave., Boston, Ma. 02130

The Daughters of St. Paul are an international congregation of religious women
serving the Church with the communications media.

ARCO/Ken Waugh

"I come from a distant country, but am always so close through the communion in the Christian faith and tradition."

Ward Wells

A Treasured Day

On January 5, 1981, the New Year of 1981 in Alaska was sparked by a ray of hope that Pope John Paul II might visit Anchorage en route from Tokyo to Rome. On January 19 the spark ignited into a flame when Archbishop Paul Marcinkus called from Rome to say that the stopover visit was on.

A few hours after the Holy Father's departure from Anchorage, Chicago's John Cardinal Cody, one of three Cardinals who came for the event, described the preparations as flawless. A week later Archbishop John Roach, of St. Paul, Minnesota, and President of the National Conference of Catholic Bishops, wrote: "...I found the Anchorage visit more moving than any of the papal visits I had experienced earlier."

From behind the scenes the over eight hundred people who had in one way or another participated in the preparations beamed with pride and sighed with relief, but none more so than the small steering and coordinating committees that spent five and a half weeks in numerous meetings starting each morning with seven o'clock Mass.

What made the planning so singular was that neither the State of Alaska nor the City of Anchorage nor the Archdiocese had been involved in an event demanding such elaborate arrangements: an unprecedented crowd, equalling almost 20% of the State's total population; press credentials for 435 media representatives; the first experience of "pooling" for local television stations; an undisclosed but massive number of secret service agents; an outdoor sound system larger than any ever assembled; a traffic control pattern and free shuttle-bus service to smooth the flow of traffic.

The most vital preparatory work, however, was engendering the expectation of a truly spiritual event. The themes repeated over and over again in numerous press conferences and television interviews centered on the Holy Father's visit as a special blessing from God upon the people of Alaska. The human dimension of a charismatic international personality was not lost; nor was the air of festive celebration that should surround a joyous civic event. But all was directed to the hope that the presence of Pope John Paul would be the occasion of a profound spiritual experience.

The hope was realized beyond expectation as a respectful and reverent crowd joined as he concelebrated the Mass. Led by a two-hundred voice choir, Catholics along with people of many faiths, and even no religion, all joined in song and prayer.

The Holy Father departed quickly, though not before a brief dog-sled ride. He had seen the many faces of Alaskans, and Alaskans had heard his voice. Together we could all join him in speaking out to God with the words of Scripture: "Abba, Father."

It was a day that will long be treasured by Alaskans.

Ward Wells

The Papal Steering Committee met with workers each morning after attending 7 a.m. Mass at Holy Family Cathedral.

Monsignor Francis Cowgill, General Coordinator of the Steering Committee for papal visit.

Walter J. Hickel and Max Hodel, lay members of the Steering Committee.

Choir practice in Holy Family Cathedral.

Constructing the altar in Delaney Park.

Mike Tobin

Arturo Mari

Pope John Paul II (left) arrives at Anchorage International Airport and is welcomed by Archbishop Francis T. Hurley, Archbishop of Anchorage.

An Eskimo parka is presented to Pope John Paul II by Mrs. Clara Tiulana, Mrs. Agnes Mayac and Mrs. Maria Tyson.

Felici

Felici

William Wilson, newly named as personal representative of President Reagan to the Holy Father, meets Pope John Paul II for the first time. In center background is Raymond Donovan, U.S. Secretary of Labor, who represented the Reagan Administration.

The Holy Father greets Bishop Francis D. Gleeson, S.J., Former Bishop of Fairbanks and Bishop Michael H. Kenny, Bishop of the Diocese of Juneau, Alaska.

Felici

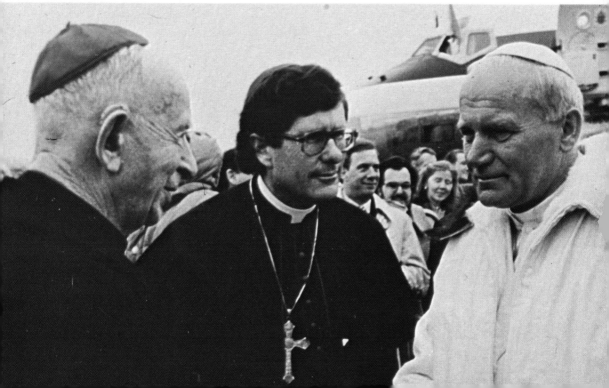

The Holy Father joins the only two brothers who serve as Catholic bishops in the United States. Mark J. Hurley, left, is Bishop of Santa Rosa, California; Francis T. Hurley, right, Archbishop of Anchorage, hosted the Papal visit.

Felici

Mike Tobin

Mike Tobin

Mike Tobin

Felici ▲

Mike Tobin ▼

ARCO/Ken Waugh

ARCO/Ken Waugh

Anchorage Daily News/Fran Durner

Mayor and Mrs. George Sullivan and Governor Jay Hammond.

Monsignor Francis Cowgill and Max Hodel, members of Steering Committee.

Mrs. Max Hodel and Mrs. Walter J. Hickel, members of Steering Committee.

Felici

Felici

Felici

Felici

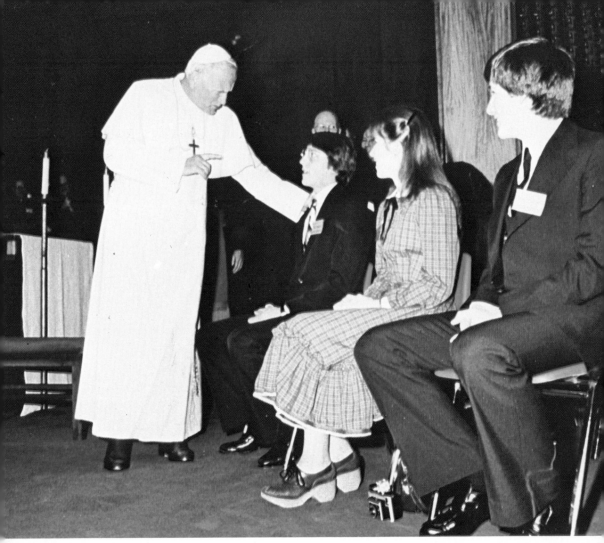

photos: Felici

Cathedral Address

"Dear brothers and sisters in Christ,

" 'I thank God whenever I think of you; and every time I pray for all of you, I pray with joy, remembering how you have helped to spread the Good News' (Phil. 1:3-4).

"These words of St. Paul express the sentiments of my heart as I greet you today here in Anchorage. Indeed, I pray with joy whenever I think of my brother priests and my brothers and sisters in religious life. *I thank God for your dedication to Christ, your presence in the Church and your collaboration in her mission.* And I thank God for your prayers, in which you unite with the whole Body of Christ in praising the name of the most Holy Trinity and in asking God's mercy for His people.

"In writing my last Encyclical, my thoughts often turned to you who in a particular way share with me the *mission of proclaiming the mercy of God to the present generation.* Every evening we pray in the Liturgy of the Hours the words of Mary: 'His mercy is from age to age on those who fear him' (Lk. 1:50). It is this truth of salvation, the truth about the mercy of God, which we must proclaim to our generation, to the men and women of our age who seem to be moving away from the mystery of God's mercy. Thus I wrote in the Encyclical, 'The Church lives an authentic life when she professes and proclaims mercy—the most stupendous attribute of the Creator and of the Redeemer—and when she brings people close to the source of the Savior's mercy, of which she is the trustee and dispenser' (*Dives in misericordia,* no. 13).

"My brothers and sisters in Christ, never doubt the vital importance of your presence in the Church, the vital importance of religious life and the ministerial priesthood in the mission of proclaiming the mercy of God. Through your daily lives, which are often accompanied by the sign of the cross, and through your faithful service and persevering hope, you show your deep faith in *God's merciful love,* and you bear witness to that *love which is more powerful than evil, and stronger than death.*

"Have confidence, therefore, in the One who called you to this life. Have confidence in God 'whose power, working in us, can do infinitely more than we can ask or imagine; glory be to him from generation to generation in the Church and in Christ Jesus for ever and ever. Amen' (Eph. 3:20-21)."

Felici

His Holiness greets Bishop Gregory of Sitka, Orthodox Bishop of Alaska.

photos: Felic

photos: Felici

Visiting the Handicapped

Raymond M. Stefun   Felici

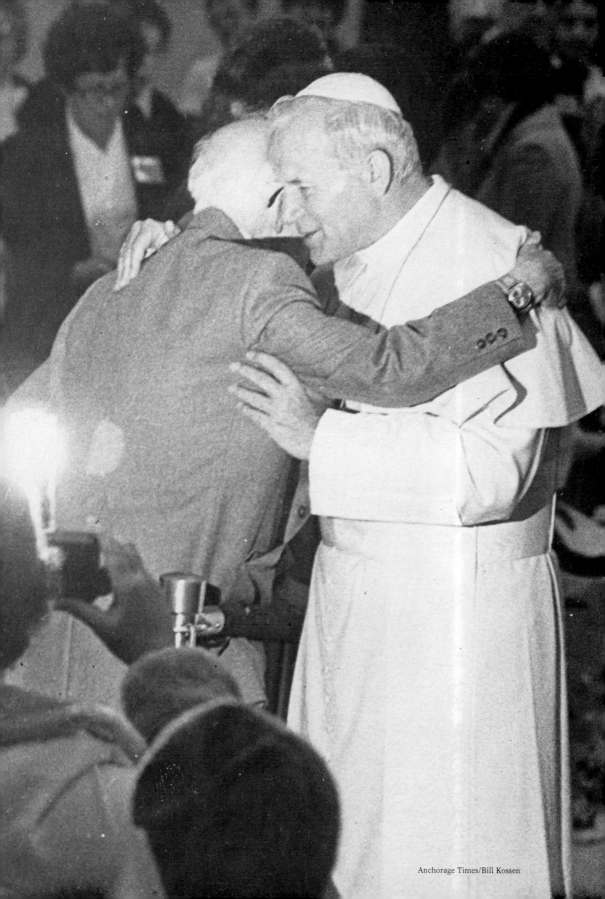

Anchorage Times/Bill Kossen

photos: Dennis Cowals

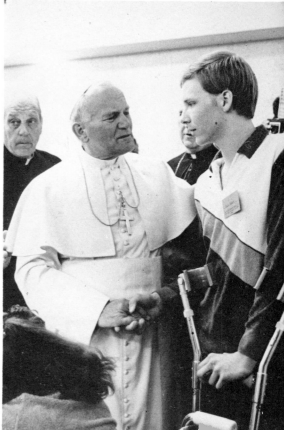

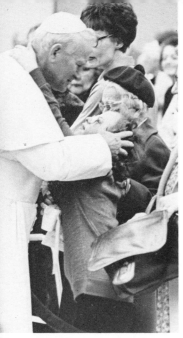

photos: Dennis Cowals

Felici

Felici

photos: Felici

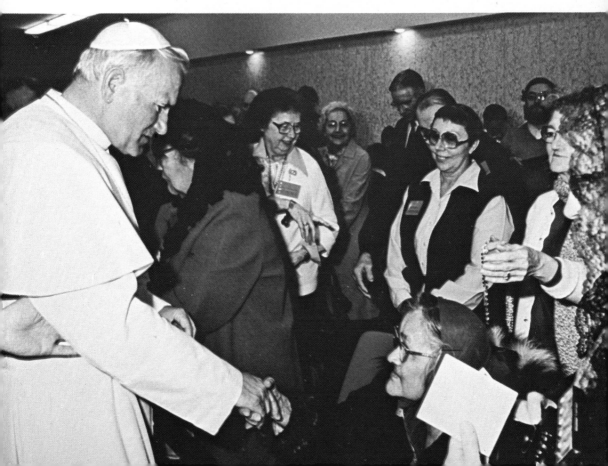

Felici

Felici

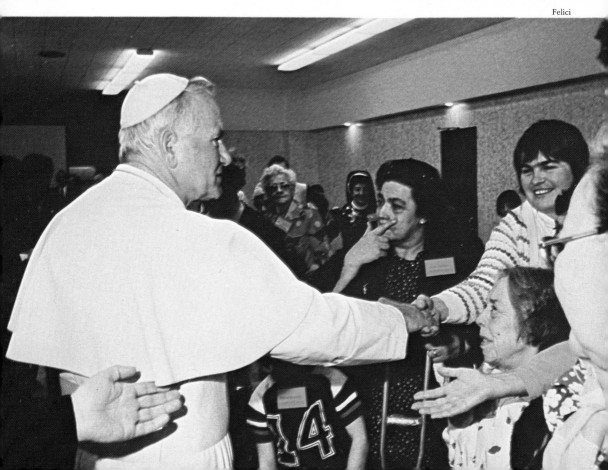

Felici

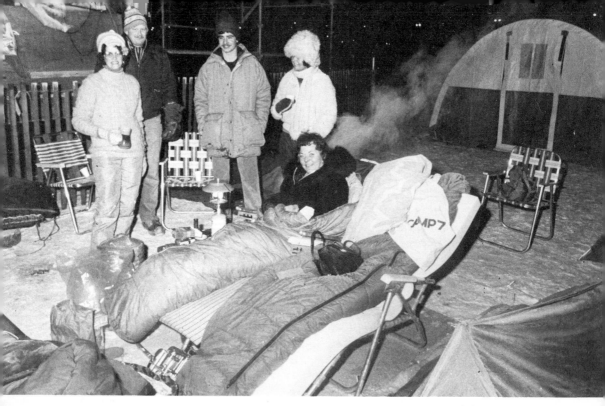

Campers pitched tents near the altar.

An early arrival sought protection from the cold.

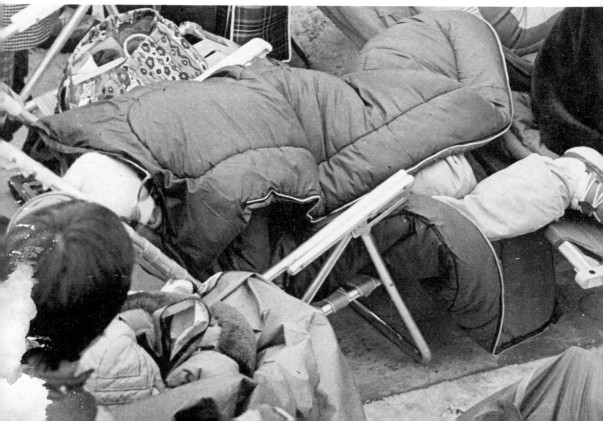

Mike Tobin

Anchorage Times

ARCO/Ken Waugh

photos: ARCO/Ken Waugh

Arturo Mari

Anchorage Times/Dave Predeger

Mike Tobin

photos: Mike Tobin

Ralph Amouak, Eskimo artist, with a crucifix for Pope John Paul II carved from walrus tusk.

The Mass in Delaney Park

Mike Tobin

Mike Tobin

Don Doll, S.J.

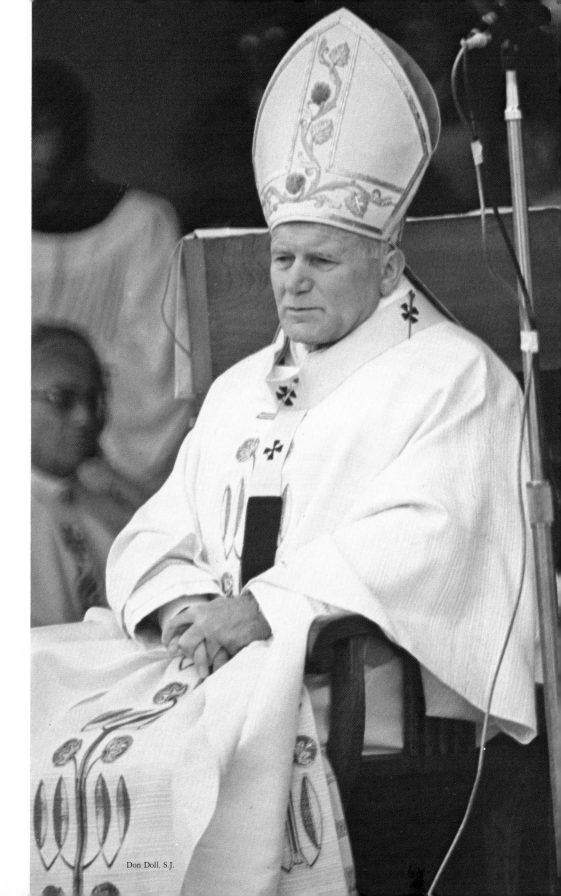

Don Doll, S.J.

Archbishop Hurley's Welcome

Don Doll, S.J.

"Your Holiness,

"As we Alaskans greet you, the words of Jesus Christ in St. Luke's gospel come to mind:

" 'I have made you a light for the nations, so that my salvation may reach the end of the earth....'

"St. Luke, Your Holiness, believed that the City of Rome qualified as 'the end of the earth.' But the vision of the Master reached far beyond the Mediterranean—so far beyond that today you, His Vicar, are truly at 'the end of the earth.' No future Pope will travel further from the Eternal City unless he chooses a spaceship to the moon, a challenge which many feel would be very tempting to Your Holiness.

"We Alaskans, however, see ourselves as only symbolically at the end of the earth. As with Rome of old, more and more roads are leading to this land of the North on the Pacific Rim, perhaps suggesting for us also a special destiny in history.

"Alaska is a land to which pioneer settlers came from both east and west. They came first from Asia over the route you have just come. Centuries later they arrived from the Western world over the route you are about to follow. Here they found a land of unexcelled beauty and natural resources. They and we, their heirs, have treasured and respected both the land and the sea. We have developed both so that today the dogsled and the jet plane symbolize not just the meeting of cultures but more the merging of human genius and industry put to the service of people.

"The location of this state is singular. Here the two great superpowers, the United States of America and the Soviet Union, share a common border. From both these nations we draw our cultural heritage, for over this land once flew the flag of Holy Russia. That heritage is a deeply religious one, rooted in the gospel message of Jesus Christ, a heritage preserved and enriched by the missionaries and the people here.

"In the context of this history we have listened to your words. You have challenged those with material resources to use their genius to feed and care for their brothers and sisters around the world, always insisting that the most precious of all resources is the human person. You have urged people of different religious traditions to cultivate their spiritual roots to bring forth unity in Jesus Christ. To the neighboring superpowers you have proclaimed the gospel as the base for peaceful coexistence, the gospel of Jesus Christ rather than the precarious balance of mutual atomic terror.

"Because of your faith in that gospel you have constantly assured us that peace is possible; peace, which is the fruit of justice; with mercy as the handmaid of justice and peace; and all based on truth.

"All those things you have said from afar, and we have listened. Today you are here among us, and we are eager to listen to any challenge you have for this land of destiny.

"Holy Father, like the Divine Master, you are among your people; faithful to His command, you are going out to all the world. You are indeed a light for all nations, a witness to the end of the earth.

"Our Blessed Lord never traveled from Jerusalem to Rome, but Peter, His Vicar, did. Peter, in turn, never traveled from Rome to Anchorage, but John Paul II, his Successor, has.

"This is indeed a day which the Lord has made, a rare date in the history of Alaska.

"We Alaskans, all of us, are profoundly grateful, and we welcome you!"

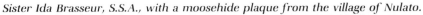

Sister Ida Brasseur, S.S.A., with a moosehide plaque from the village of Nulato.

Mike Tobin

Arturo Mari

photos: Mike Tobin

Anchorage Times/Alice Puster

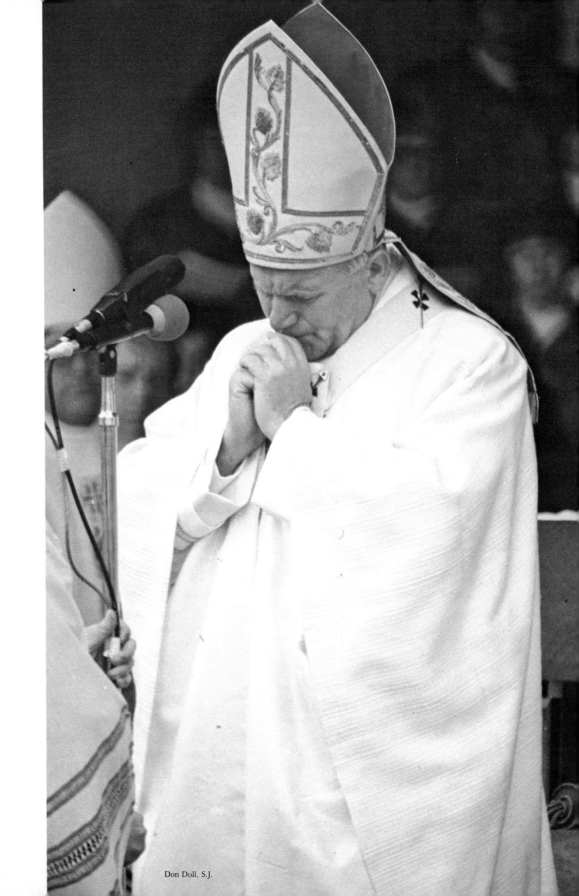

Don Doll, S.J.

Homily of Pope John Paul II

"Dear brothers and sisters,
" 'Sing to the Lord a new song;
Sing to the Lord, all the earth!
Declare his glory among the nations,
His marvelous works among all peoples!'

"The joyful sentiments that moved the heart of the Psalmist to praise the Lord in these words are the same sentiments that well up within us as we gather here in Anchorage to celebrate this Mass of the Holy Spirit. What better way could we express praise to God than *in that Spirit who is the vital principle of the Church's life?* What more fitting song could be sung than one that tells of the Holy Spirit's inspiration and guidance in proclaiming the gospel of Christ to the world? What else gives so much cause for rejoicing as the indwelling of the Spirit that is for us a pledge, a foretaste, a guarantee of the glory that awaits us in heaven?

"Being here in Alaska, so richly endowed with the beauties of nature, at once so rugged and yet so splendid, *we sense the presence of God's Spirit in the manifold handiwork of creation.* And not only do we feel this presence in inanimate nature and in the order of plants and animals, but all the more so in the precious gift of life which God has breathed into each one of His sons and daughters. Having fashioned man and woman in His own image, God remains with each individual on the pilgrimage of this earthly life, inviting, calling, prompting through His Spirit an acceptance of the salvation offered in Christ.

"As I look out over this gathering here, I see the evidence of the Holy Spirit's call of faith in Alaska. Here *many peoples of diverse backgrounds and cultures are drawn into one community of faith.* Here native Alaskans—Eskimos, Aleuts, and Indians—join together with people from all parts of the United States to form one ecclesial community. Here in recent years Hispanics have come in increasing numbers to join in the united fellowship of the Church. In acknowledging this activity of the Spirit, are we not impelled to make a joyful song to the Lord? Do not our hearts overflow in speaking of all the wonderful blessings that the Spirit has infused into the Church?

"But there is another reason for giving thanks to the Holy Spirit in this hour. Having now completed a pastoral journey during these past eleven days that took me to Pakistan, the Philippines, Guam, Japan and now here in Alaska, I wish to express profound gratitude to the Holy Spirit for His guidance and protection throughout this visit. In the name of the most Holy Trinity, I began my journey as a pilgrim of faith, responding to the charge that Jesus gave to Peter: 'Strengthen your brothers' (Lk. 22:32). It was to fulfill this responsibility, which through the working of the Holy Spirit had been entrusted to me, that I undertook this journey, and I hope that with the assistance of the same Holy Spirit these efforts will be a source of encouragement for the bishops and for all my brothers and sisters in the Faith.

"We may well ask: How does the Spirit move human hearts to respond to the revelation of the Lord's glory? Jesus tells us in the Gospel today that the mysteries of faith are hidden from the learned and clever of this world and made known instead to mere children. The response of faith is always a child-like response—one that acknowledges God as Father.

"Jesus Himself teaches us this lesson when He accepts His life's mission, not seeking to do His own will but rather the will of the One who sent Him (cf. Jn. 5:30). Conceived by the power of the Holy Spirit, Jesus is the bearer of the Spirit in every situation of His public ministry. When He has fulfilled the will of His Father in His passion, death and resurrection, Jesus sends the Holy Spirit upon His disciples in order to continue and to bring to completion the Father's universal plan of salvation.

"It is well for us to reflect for a few moments on what is implied in *the Sonship of Christ,* in which we share through the Holy Spirit. In this respect, our second reading from St. Paul's Letter to the Romans is of great benefit. The Apostle describes the status of a son as being distinct from the condition of a slave. There is a different relationship—one of intimacy—and this intimacy is indicated in the name by which the Father is known and addressed. St. Paul tells us that those who are born of water and the Holy Spirit speak to the Divine Father in the very words which Jesus used in the intimacy of His prayer in Gethsemane: 'Abba, Father' (cf. Rom. 8:16). Our sonship in Christ, then, involves a relationship that is closer and more personal than that of a child to the parent who has generated life. On the part of the Father there is a love 'which not only creates the good but also grants participation in the very life of God: Father, Son and Holy Spirit' (*Dives in misericordia,* no. 7). While the slave had an obligation to the master, the son is free and can thus return the very love by which he has been loved.

"As children of God, our love, given and sustained in the Holy Spirit, invites us over and over again into a deeper intimacy with the Father. And how willing and enthusiastic should be our response! This invitation is perceived in prayer—which is not just a duty to be performed but also a means of strengthening our union in love. This activity of prayer in the Church is never limited to certain groups or particular individuals. It is a privilege and duty for all. Nor should prayer be limited to participation in the liturgical prayer of the Church; it should also reflect the constant search of individuals or groups to discover in private and communal prayer ways of deepening their union with Christ.

"In this context we can recognize the wisdom of Paul VI, who observed that it is through prayer that Christians attain the first fruit of the Spirit, which is joy: 'The Holy Spirit raises up therein a filial prayer that springs from the depths of the soul and is expressed in praise, thanksgiving, reparation, and supplication. Then we can experience joy which is properly spiritual, the joy which is a fruit of the Holy Spirit. It consists in the human spirit's finding repose and deep satisfaction in possession of the Triune God, known by faith and loved with the charity that comes from Him' (*Gaudete in Domino*, III).

"The presence of this joy, however, does not exclude the possibility of suffering. St. Paul readily points this out when he says that *a share in Christ's sonship means to share also in His suffering.* For to glory in Christ is to glory in His cross (cf. Gal. 6:14). If we seek to deepen our relationship with the Father in the Holy Spirit, then we should not be surprised to find that we are misunderstood, opposed or even persecuted for our beliefs.

"Nine days ago I beatified Lorenzo Ruiz and his companions in the Philippines. These holy men and women knew well the meaning of Christ's words: 'If they persecuted me, they will persecute you' (Jn. 15:20). But despite the opposition they encountered, they trusted in the guidance of the Holy Spirit to sustain them in the face of suffering.

"Such faith has also marked the history of *the missionaries in these Alaskan territories.* They too met the cross in the form of physical limitations, disappointments and opposition in their efforts to spread the Faith. Often their endeavors seemed to bear little results in their own lifetime, but the seeds were planted for the witness of a faith that is in evidence today.

"Dear brothers and sisters, let us learn the wisdom of the children of God to trust and hope in the abiding presence of the Holy Spirit in the Church. May we never be confounded by the suffering that may come into our lives, but seek rather to transform it in the light of the cross of our Savior Jesus Christ. May our confidence always be in the Holy Spirit in order to discover in each new situation an opportunity to extend Christ's redemptive love.

"*The present generation brings with it new challenges and new opportunities for the Church in Alaska.* The Gospel needs to be proclaimed anew every day, and the fire of faith needs to be fanned into flame. The Church needs someone to preach, to teach and administer the sacraments of Christ's love. I do not hesitate to ask the youth of Alaska to respond to this challenge. Among your numbers, the Holy Spirit is surely sowing seeds of priestly and religious vocations. Do not stifle that call, but give yourselves generously to the service of Christ's Gospel.

"At the same time, the Holy Spirit has spoken through the Second Vatican Council of a need for increased involvement of the laity in the apostolate of the Church. In the varying circumstances of their lives, lay persons are called to participate in the Church's mission. In their families and in their daily occupations, in works of mercy and charity, in catechesis and the cause of justice, lay men and women must build up the Church and help consecrate the world. Each member of the Church has a special charism that the Spirit of God has given for the good of the Church. Each gift must be used to benefit the entire Body of Christ.

"My dear friends in Christ, let us never cease praising *the Holy Spirit,* who is the inexhaustible source of our life in Christ. He was present to the Church on the first Pentecost. He remains with the Church today and for ever. Let us be confident in His strengthening power and learn to be ever docile in following His ways. Let us be increasingly sensitive to His influence on our actions and always ready to pray for His divine assistance:

" 'Come, Holy Spirit, fill the hearts of your faithful
And enkindle in them the fire of your love.
Send forth your Spirit and they shall be created
and you will renew the face of the earth. Amen.' "

Mike Tobin

Brother George Feltes of Fairbanks, an Alaskan Jesuit for 51 years, receives Communion from the Holy Father.

DSP

Seven-year-old Travis Rose of Skagway receives his First Communion from Pope John Paul II.

Anchorage Daily News/Fran Durner

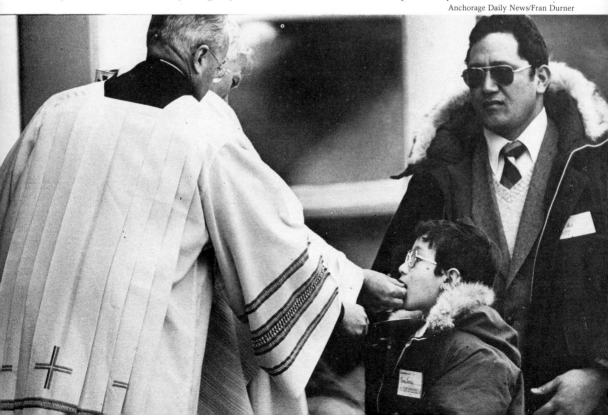

Mike Tobin

Mike Tobin

Don Doll, S.J

Thomas W. Gregory

Eskimo Deacons from western and Arctic Alaska assisted in the Papal Mass.

The Holy Father's Homily is interpreted for the deaf.

ARCO/Ken Waugh

Mike Tobin

Anchorage Daily News

nchorage awaits the pope

The visit of John P

Pope hails diversity, beauty of Alaska in park

Pope's visit closes streets

Pope's itinerary will keep him busy

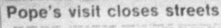
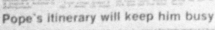

weather   **index**

er housing, food costs push
of inflation down to 9.1 percent

Economic report sparks capital move battle

Mike Tobin

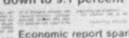

AN ANCHORAGE DAY IN HISTORY

The Pope i

A SPECIAL SECTION
The Pope in Alaska
Section B

Remember the day . . . .

Inside, a special keepsake pictorial
section preserving the pope's visit

Anchorage Daily News

The Anchorage

Anchorage had a

Thousands greet John Paul

● Being here in Alaska, so richly
endowed with the beauties of
nature, at once so rugged and
yet so splendid, we sense the
presence of God's Spirit

Barbara Millsap saw more than pope

index   weather

Thatcher: El Salvador off-li

Polar Sea may stay in ice

POPE JOHN PAUL II
man, message, mission

We
Ala

● Climbing
it's kid stuff
● The lucky li
of Nancy H
● Networking
the new g

The
Archbishop
of Anchorage

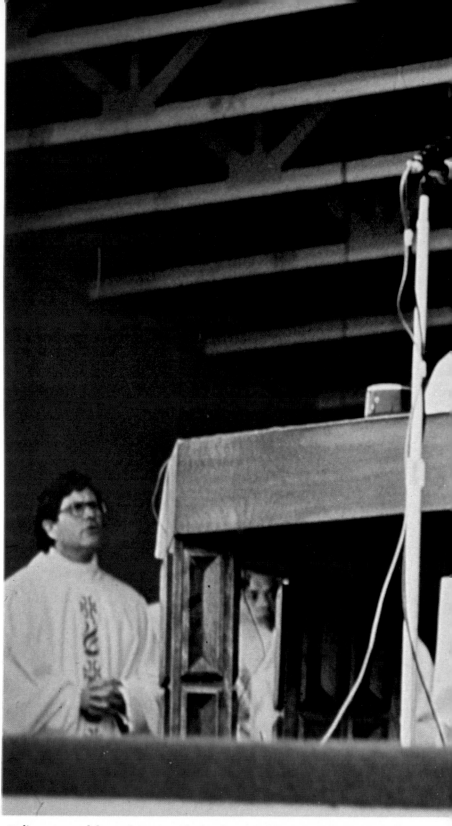

His Holiness concelebrated Mass with the three Bishops of Alaska at his side. From left: Bishop Michael H. Kenny of Juneau, Archbishop Francis T. Hurley of Anchorage, and Bishop Robert L. Whelan, S.J., of Fairbanks, far right.

Fr. Tero

Jesuit Father Rene Astruc, center, assists Beverly Michaels and John Valentine of KIMO-TV in describing the Mass for a statewide audience.

Felici

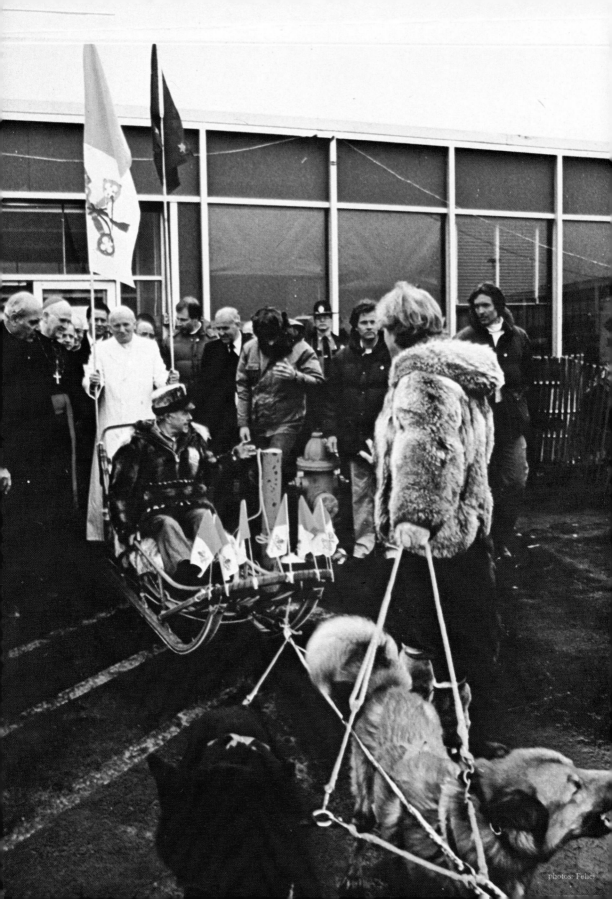

Farewell

"Dear friends,

"I am happy that, on my return to Rome from my pastoral visit to the Philippines, Guam and Japan, I have been able to stop here in Anchorage. It has been a joy to spend these few hours in your midst, to meet the people of Alaska and above all to celebrate the Eucharist with my brothers and sisters of the Catholic Faith.

"At this time I want to thank you for the kind reception and warm hospitality which you have extended to me, and I am grateful to all those who generously assisted in the planning and organization of this day. Permit me also to add a special word of gratitude to President Reagan who has sent a personal delegation to meet me here in Anchorage.

"Before continuing my journey, may I take this occasion to extend my greetings to all the citizens of the United States of America. This brief stop in Alaska and the cordial welcome accorded to me here brings to mind my previous pastoral visit to your country, the memory of which I still hold dear. I pray that God will bless you and your families.

"And now as I leave Alaska to complete the last part of this pastoral journey which has taken me around the world, my thoughts turn to God and to His praises expressed in the words of the Psalmist: 'O Lord, our Lord, how glorious is your name over all the earth!' (Ps. 8:2)"

Anchorage Times/Dave Predeger

TALKS OF POPE JOHN PAUL II

Africa—Apostolic Pilgrimage
Compiled and indexed by the Daughters of St. Paul
> Contains all 72 talks of John Paul II during his ten-day visit to the people of Africa in 1980.
> Thought-provoking for all the People of God. 52 photos in color and black and white. 432 pages; cloth $8.00; paper $7.00 — EP0025

Brazil—Journey in the Light of the Eucharist
Compiled and indexed by the Daughters of St. Paul
> The complete collection of the talks given by His Holiness during his trip to Brazil in 1980. 412 pages; cloth $8.00; paper $7.00 — EP0175

France—Message of Peace, Trust, Love and Faith
Compiled and indexed by the Daughters of St. Paul
> The 28 addresses in the Pope's four-day visit to France in 1980, a "country of glorious tradition." 37 photographs; 250 pages; cloth $5.00; paper $3.50 — EP0488

Germany, Pilgrimage of Unity and Peace
Compiled and indexed by the Daughters of St. Paul
> The celebration of the seventh centenary of the death of the German-born St. Albert the Great in 1980 gave the Holy Father the occasion to honor Germany's valuable contribution to the spiritual heritage of the Church and of the whole of humanity. 288 pages; cloth $6.00; paper $5.00 — EP0515

I Believe in Youth, Christ Believes in Youth
Compiled and indexed by the Daughters of St. Paul
> A second volume of the Pope's talks to youth. 304 pages; cloth $4.95; paper $3.95 — EP0586

Ireland—In the Footsteps of St. Patrick
Compiled and indexed by the Daughters of St. Paul
> The historic three-day visit to Ireland is recaptured in this collection of 22 talks given by His Holiness from September 29 to October 1, 1979. 150 pages; cloth $3.95; paper $2.95 — EP0675

Pilgrim to Poland
Compiled and indexed by the Daughters of St. Paul
> A collection of the Holy Father's 41 talks given during his heartwarming visit to his native Poland in 1979. 54 photographs in color and black and white. 290 pages; cloth $5.00; paper $3.50 — EP0955

Pope John Paul II—He Came to Us As a Father
Compiled by the Daughters of St. Paul
> This unique book of memories captures in over 400 photographs the warmth and spirituality of the pastoral visit of Pope John Paul II to the United States, from October 1-7, 1979. Key excerpts from His Holiness' talks enrich this volume: An unforgettable message for all Americans. 256 pages; cloth $14.95 — EP0957

Puebla—A Pilgrimage of Faith

Compiled by the Daughters of St. Paul

The 36 talks given during His Holiness' Latin American pilgrimage in 1979. 208 pages; cloth $3.00; paper $2.00 — EP0976

Servant of Truth—Messages of John Paul II

Compiled and indexed by the Daughters of St. Paul

The full text of 130 addresses given from December, 1978, to March, 1979, including His Holiness' talks at Puebla and his first encyclical, the Redeemer of Man. 44 photographs in color and black and white. 578 pages; cloth $9.95; paper $8.95 — RA0164

Talks of John Paul II

With Foreword by His Eminence, John Cardinal Krol

Compiled and indexed by the Daughters of St. Paul

109 addresses, from October 16, 1978, to the end of December. The addresses are presented in their entirety. 17 four-color photographs; 35 black and white photographs. 542 pages; cloth $7.95; paper $6.95 — RA0188

Turkey—Ecumenical Pilgrimage

Compiled and indexed by the Daughters of St. Paul

All the addresses of His Holiness given in Turkey during his two-day visit in 1979, as well as the Joint Declaration signed by His Holiness and by the Ecumenical Patriarch, Dimitrios I, whose address is also included. 112 pages; cloth $3.50; paper $2.50 — EP1085

U.S.A.—The Message of Justice, Peace and Love

Compiled and indexed by the Daughters of St. Paul

Complete collection of the talks given by His Holiness during his historic visit to America, October 1-7, 1979: Boston, New York, Philadelphia, Des Moines, Chicago, Washington.

What did the Vicar of Christ tell America wherever he went? A book to treasure, to meditate, to live by. 320 pages; cloth $5.95; paper $4.95 — EP1095

Visible Signs of the Gospel

Compiled and indexed by the Daughters of St. Paul

Messages on consecrated life—faith, warmth and encouragement vibrate from the Pope's every word. 308 pages; cloth $4.00; paper $2.95 — EP1098

The Whole Truth About Man

Edited and with an introduction by Rev. James V. Schall, S.J.

Indexed by the Daughters of St. Paul

The Holy Father's talks to university faculties and students. 354 pages; cloth $7.95; paper $6.95 — EP1099

"You Are My Favorites"

Pope John Paul II to children

Edited by the Daughters of St. Paul

In this colorful book, full of pictures and photographs, the Pope speaks to all the children of the world. He tells them about Jesus, faith, love, truth, school, holidays, sports, the Gospel, and much, much more. 192 pages; cloth $6.95 — EP1125

"You Are the Future, You Are My Hope"

Compiled and indexed by the Daughters of St. Paul

Volume one of talks of His Holiness *to young people* of all ages. Reveals the stirring personal appeal of the Pope to the new generation. Excellent for youth and those involved in guidance. 326 pages; 16 pages of full-color photos; cloth $4.95; paper $3.95 — EP1120

INQUIRE about upcoming volumes of the Pope's talks on the priesthood, human life, the social order, family life, and catechesis on the Book of Genesis, etc.

ENCYCLICAL LETTERS AND OTHER MESSAGES OF POPE JOHN PAUL II

Address of Pope John Paul II to the General Assembly of the United Nations
October 2, 1979. 20 pages; 30¢ — EP0005

Apostolic Exhortation on Catechesis in Our Time *(Catechesi Tradendae)*
The Holy Father's guidelines for handing on the Faith today. Given on October 16, 1979. 68 pages; 60¢ — EP0285

The Freedom of Conscience and Religion
September 1, 1980. 12 pages; 35¢ — EP0480

Instruction Concerning Worship of the Eucharistic Mystery
Given in April, 1980. 16 pages; 25¢ — EP0605

Letter to All Bishops of the Church and to All Priests
Issued on Holy Thursday, 1979. 34 pages; 25¢ — EP0688

On the Mercy of God *(Dives in Misericordia)*
52 pages; 50¢ — EP0863

On the Mystery and Worship of the Eucharist *(Dominicae Cenae)*
Issued on February 24, 1980. 40 pages; 35¢ — EP0895

The Redeemer of Man
The encyclical letter, *Redemptor hominis,* March 4, 1979, the first of His Holiness' pontificate. 64 pages; 50¢ — EP0978

POPE JOHN PAUL II ON CASSETTE

Boston, October 1, 1979
Welcome, Logan Airport; To Priests, Holy Cross Cathedral; Homily, Boston Common. 60 min., $4.95 — CSM0310

New York, October 2, 1979
Welcome, LaGuardia Airport; To International and Non-governmental Organizations, UN; To journalists, UN; To UN staff members; Farewell message to UN. 36 min., $4.50 — CSM2642

Address of His Holiness, Pope John Paul II, to the United Nations. 60 min., $4.95 — CSM0030

New York, October 2, 1979
Welcome, St. Patrick's Cathedral; Homily, Yankee Stadium. 35 min., $4.50 — CSM2640

New York, October 2, 1979
Address, Harlem; Address, South Bronx (Spanish). 15 min., $4.00 — CSM2643

New York, October 3, 1979
Homily, Morning Prayer, St. Patrick's Cathedral; To Youth, Madison Square Garden; Address, Battery Park; Address, Shea Stadium. 28 min., $4.25 — CSM2641

Philadelphia, October 3, 1979
Welcome, Cathedral Basilica of Sts. Peter and Paul; Homily, Logan Circle. 40 min., $4.50 — CSM3050

Philadelphia, October 4, 1979
Address, Immaculate Conception; Ukrainian Cathedral. 15 min., $4.00 — CSM3051

Philadelphia, October 4, 1979
Homily, Civic Center. 36 min., $4.50 — CSM3052

Des Moines, October 4, 1979
Homily, Living History Farms. 30 min., $4.25 — CSM0630

Chicago, October 4, 1979
To religious brothers. 20 min., $4.00 — CSM0430

Chicago, October 5, 1979
Homily, Grant Park. 30 min., $4.25 — CSM0431

Washington, D.C., October 6, 1979
Addresses of the President and the Pope at the White House. 40 min., $4.50 — CSM4110

Washington, D.C., October 6, 1979
Address to Organization of American States (Spanish and English). 30 min., $4.25 — CSM4111

Washington, D.C., October 7, 1979
To Women Religious, Shrine of the Immaculate Conception. 40 min., $4.50 — CSM3775

Washington, D.C., October 7, 1979
To Students, outside the Shrine of the Immaculate Conception; To Theologians and Catholic Educators, Catholic University of America. 25 min., $4.25 — CSM3770

Washington, D.C., October 7, 1979
Homily, Capitol Mall. 30 min., $4.25 — CSM1510

ALSO AVAILABLE:

Pope John Paul II Visits Anchorage
February 26, 1981. $4.95 — CSM3880

Please order from addresses on the following page, specifying title and item number.

Daughters of St. Paul

IN MASSACHUSETTS
   50 St. Paul's Ave. Jamaica Plain, Boston, MA 02130;
      617-522-8911; 617-522-0875;
   172 Tremont Street, Boston, MA 02111; **617-426-5464;**
      617-426-4230
IN NEW YORK
   78 Fort Place, Staten Island, NY 10301; **212-447-5071**
   59 East 43rd Street, New York, NY 10017; **212-986-7580**
   7 State Street, New York, NY 10004; **212-447-5071**
   625 East 187th Street, Bronx, NY 10458; **212-584-0440**
   525 Main Street, Buffalo, NY 14203; **716-847-6044**
IN NEW JERSEY
   Hudson Mall — Route 440 and Communipaw Ave.,
      Jersey City, NJ 07304; **201-433-7740**
IN CONNECTICUT
   202 Fairfield Ave., Bridgeport, CT 06604; **203-335-9913**
IN OHIO
   2105 Ontario St. (at Prospect Ave.), Cleveland, OH 44115; **216-621-9427**
   25 E. Eighth Street, Cincinnati, OH 45202; **513-721-4838**
IN PENNSYLVANIA
   1719 Chestnut Street, Philadelphia, PA 19103; **215-568-2638**
IN FLORIDA
   2700 Biscayne Blvd., Miami, FL 33137; **305-573-1618**
IN LOUISIANA
   4403 Veterans Memorial Blvd., Metairie, LA 70002; **504-887-7631;**
      504-887-0113
   1800 South Acadian Thruway, P.O. Box 2028, Baton Rouge, LA 70821
      504-343-4057; 504-343-3814
IN MISSOURI
   1001 Pine Street (at North 10th), St. Louis, MO 63101; **314-621-0346;**
      314-231-1034
IN ILLINOIS
   172 North Michigan Ave., Chicago, IL 60601; **312-346-4228;**
      312-346-3240
IN TEXAS
   114 Main Plaza, San Antonio, TX 78205; **512-224-8101**
IN CALIFORNIA
   1570 Fifth Avenue, San Diego, CA 92101; **714-232-1442**
   46 Geary Street, San Francisco, CA 94108; **415-781-5180**
IN HAWAII
   1143 Bishop Street, Honolulu, HI 96813; **808-521-2731**
IN ALASKA
   750 West 5th Avenue, Anchorage AK 99501; **907-272-8183**
IN CANADA
   3022 Dufferin Street, Toronto 395, Ontario, Canada
IN ENGLAND
   128, Notting Hill Gate, London W11 3QG, England
   133 Corporation Street, Birmingham B4 6PH, England
   5A-7 Royal Exchange Square, Glasgow G1 3AH, England
   82 Bold Street, Liverpool L1 4HR, England
IN AUSTRALIA
   58 Abbotsford Rd., Homebush, N.S.W., Sydney 2140, Australia

Don Doll, S.J.